ONE OF FOUR MURALS FROM THE SALON OF THE JAS DE BOUFFAN, 1859

The Jas de Bouffan was generally in a poor state of repair when the Cézanne family moved there, and Paul was given permission to paint on the walls of one of the rooms. In 1859 Cézanne painted a series of murals of the four seasons. These paintings are the earliest known works of Cézanne. The elongated female figures depicted in the murals show Cézanne's knowledge of art of previous generations. They show the distinct influence of artists such as the 16th-century Italian Sandro Botticelli, and Cézanne himself recognises his debt by signing the paintings, not in his own name, but that of Ingres, who was famed for his academic style.

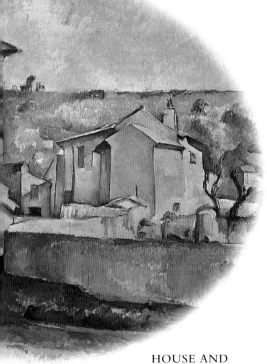

HOUSE AND FARM AT THE JAS DE BOUFFAN *(detail)*, 1885/7

In 1859 Louis-Auguste Cézanne purchased a fine 18th-century house with surrounding grounds situated close to the centre of Aix. The house had formerly belonged to the Governor of Provence and was called the *Jas de Bouffan* (House of the Wind).

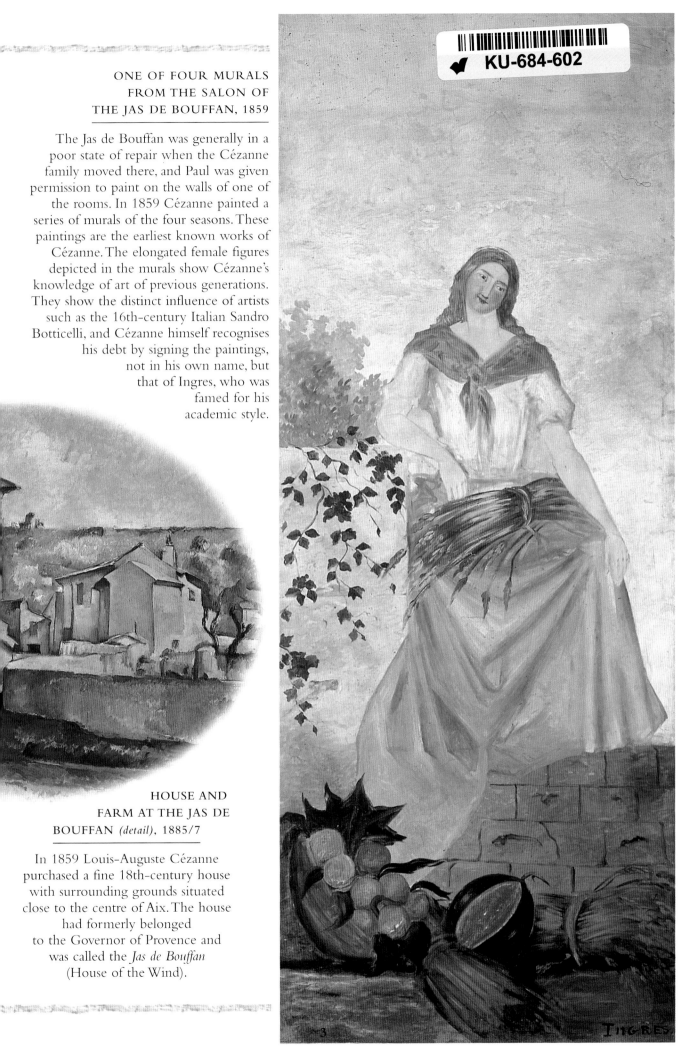

INGRES

INFLUENCES & EARLY WORKS

*I*n 1862 Cézanne settled in Paris. Like all aspiring artists he was a frequent visitor to the Louvre where he spent hours sitting in front of paintings meticulously copying the great masters. This was the established way of learning how to paint and Cézanne was no exception. Gradually he discovered the works of living artists such as Eugène Delacroix who was a great source of inspiration for artists of Cézanne's generation. Delacroix symbolised rebellion against the Classical art which dominated the art schools at the time, led by the great French artist and master draughtsman Jean Auguste Dominique Ingres. The Romantic artists, led by Delacroix, considered colour to be more important than draughtsmanship and favoured exotic subject matter over the traditional subjects depicted by the followers of Ingres. The École des Beaux-Arts taught in the Classical tradition still favoured by the critics and by the public, but it was increasingly out of touch with the new generation of artists. The up-and-coming painters no longer sought the advice and approval of the established system of teaching and they were becoming dissatisfied with the official annual exhibition of paintings at the Salon.

THE STRANGLED WOMAN
(*detail*), *c*.1870/2

In his early works painted during the 1860s Cézanne's rapid fusion of brushstrokes and colour borrow from the work of Delacroix, but also appear similar to the pictures of Honoré Daumier, an artist whose cartoons were full of biting political satire. The dark earthy realism of his solid figures could equally owe a debt to Gustave Courbet whose work would have been known to the young Cézanne. Cézanne experimented with different painterly styles during this period just as he chose to depict a wide range of subject matter, from imaginary scenes of violence to still life.

APOTHEOSIS OF DELACROIX, *c*.1870/2

Cézanne made his palette of colours deliberately bright in emulation of Delacroix. Of colour he said; '*Pure drawing is an abstraction. Line and modelling do not count; drawing and outline are not distinct, since everything in nature has colour... by the very fact of painting one draws. The accuracy of tone gives simultaneously the light and shape of the object, and the more harmonious the colour, the more the drawing becomes precise.*'

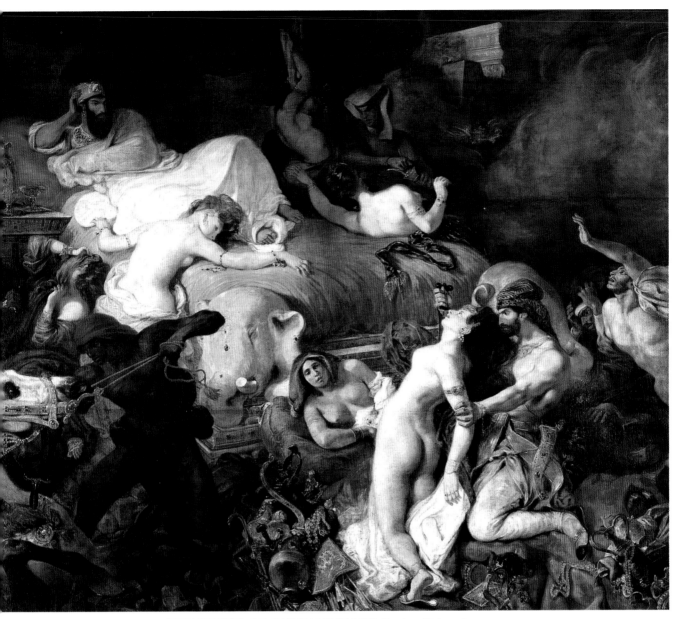

THE DEATH OF SARDANAPALUS *Eugène Delacroix*

When Delacroix painted this picture in 1829 he was angrily attacked by the art establishment for his use of brilliant colour, exotic and dramatic subject matter, and free handling of the paint, which was seen to be 'anti-French' in its rejection of French Classicism. In 1832 he visited north Africa and this opened up a whole new field of subject matter as well as heightening his appreciation of colour. He also used literary sources of inspiration including Byron, Scott and Shakespeare, and his way of painting broke new ground enabling the Realist artists to follow.

Cézanne made a number of copies of Delacroix's paintings as well as making his own pictures which also contained images of violence such as *The Abduction*, *The Murder* and *The Woman Strangled* and *The Autopsy*.

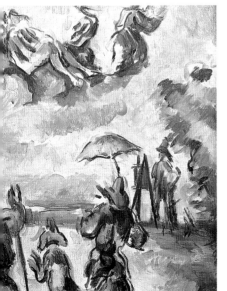

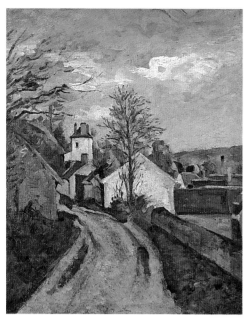

THE HOUSE OF
DR GACHET AT AUVERS, *c*.1873

Cézanne was encouraged by Pissarro to move to a small village near Pontoise called Auvers-sur-Oise. Cézanne stayed with the eccentric art enthusiast Dr. Gachet who was a great supporter of the young artists. Pissarro and Cézanne painted landscapes in the pretty countryside.

INFLUENCES & EARLY WORKS

*I*n Paris, Cézanne mixed with the most modern, adventurous painters and intellectuals who discussed their ideas about art and literature in the Paris cafés, particularly the Café Guerbois in the Batignolles district of Paris. The painter Camille Pissarro became a good friend and introduced Cézanne to artists such as Manet, Monet and Renoir. Cézanne however did not feel at ease in this company, and complained in a letter *'I am just wasting my time in every respect... just don't go imagining that I shall become a Parisian...'* In 1863 the 'Salon des Refusés' was set up to give the public the opportunity to see the works of artists rejected from the official Salon.

The picture that caused the greatest sensation at the Salon des Refusés was *Le Déjeuner sur l'Herbe* by Édouard Manet. The works of Manet and Courbet attempted to be true to life, depicting ordinary scenes of everyday life, *'bringing art into contact with the common people.'* Cézanne submitted a number of paintings to the Salon, all of which were rejected.

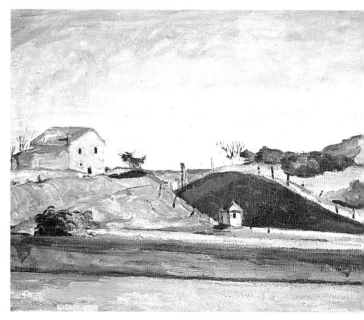

THE CUTTING, 1870

Cézanne travelled between Paris and his family home in Aix. In 1869 he met his future wife, Hortense Fiquet, who modelled for him when he was working in Paris, and they began living together. In 1870 they moved to the fishing village of L'Estaque, near Marseilles, to avoid the Franco-Prussian war. Cézanne became obsessed with painting the rocky Mediterranean landscape. Around this time he painted the landscape of a railway cutting near Aix. In the distance, behind the cutting, towers the Mont Sainte-Victoire, this feature of the Aix countryside was to dominate Cézanne's painting for the rest of his life.

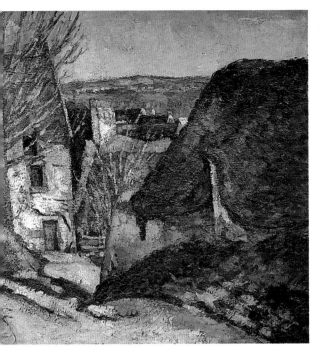

THE HOUSE OF THE HANGED MAN

This painting was made in 1873 when Cézanne was heavily influenced by the Impressionist style. The painting reveals Cézanne's continuing obsession with representing solidity of form. Heavy brushstrokes give it a physicality anchoring the imagery in the landscape, rather than relying on colour to depict light, as in the works of the Impressionist painters. *The House of the Hanged Man* was exhibited at the first Impressionist exhibition where it was purchased by Count Armand Doria for the sum of 300 francs.

PHOTO OF PISSARRO & CÉZANNE

Camille Pissarro (left) had been friends with Cézanne since they first met in Paris at the Académie Suisse in 1861. Pissarro, who was 10 years older than Cézanne, persuaded him to try painting outdoors. This *en plein air* way of painting was favoured by Pissarro and became the hallmark of the Impressionist painters. They believed it was essential to get close to their subjects, to capture what they saw with immediacy. They concerned themselves with the fleeting effects of light on the subject, and rejected the studio-bound method of painting. Pissarro had a profound influence on Cézanne's painting in the early 1870s and was equally influential on other painters of the day. Pissarro was the only artist to exhibit in all eight Impressionist exhibitions.

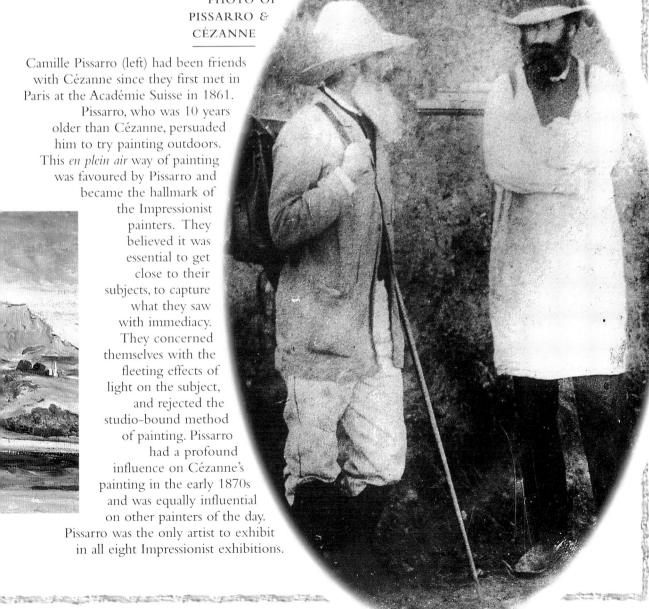

THE LIFE OF CÉZANNE

~1839~
Paul Cézanne born on the 19 January in Aix-en-Provence, eldest of three children

~1844~
Paul's parents, Louis-Auguste Cézanne and Anne-Élisabeth Aubert are married

~1852~
Attends the Collège Bourbon where he meets Émile Zola and Jean Baptiste Baille. The three become best friends

~1857~
Attends the drawing school in Aix

~1859~
Attends the University of Aix to study law

~1861~
Spends the summer in Paris studying art at the Académie Suisse where he meets Pissarro

Reluctantly returns to Aix to work in the family bank

~1862~
Cézanne gives up work and his legal studies to return to Paris with a modest allowance from his father

~1863~
Attends the Académie Suisse once more and meets Impressionist painters Sisley, Monet and Renoir

~1866~
Submits work to the Paris Salon but is rejected

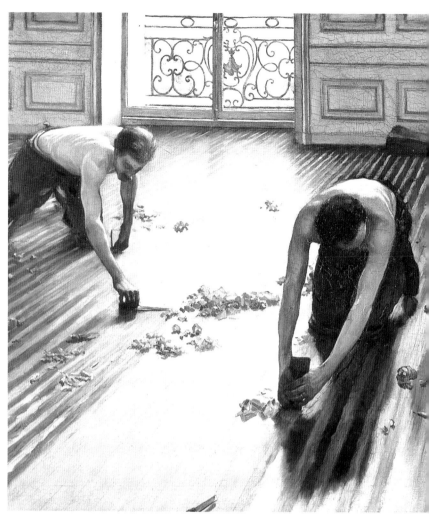

THE FLOOR STRIPPERS *Gustave Caillebotte*

La Deuxième Exposition (The Second Exhibition) of Impressionism was held at the art dealer Durand-Ruel's gallery at 11 rue le Peletier in Paris from 11 April to 9 May 1876. One of the paintings that caused the greatest sensation was *The Floor Strippers* by Gustave Caillebotte. Caillebotte was an extremely talented and wealthy artist. He extended his interest in painting not only by buying artwork, but by exhibiting it alongside his own . This painting depicts workmen stripping the floor of his new Paris apartment.

FOUR GIRLS ON A BRIDGE

Edvard Munch

Artists from all over the world flocked to Paris in the 1870s and 1880s as its reputation as a vibrant exciting city with the most modern trends in art spread. Wealthy Americans travelled to Paris, some to collect this new art, some to become artists themselves. A young Norwegian painter named Edvard Munch travelled to Paris and much of his formative youth was spent in the city. By 1892 Munch had attracted enough interest to be able to hold a large Exhibition of his work in Berlin. His art was very influential and he soon became a powerful factor in the growth of the Expressionist movement. Munch had himself been influenced in Paris by the deeply personal vision expressed in the works of Gauguin and van Gogh.

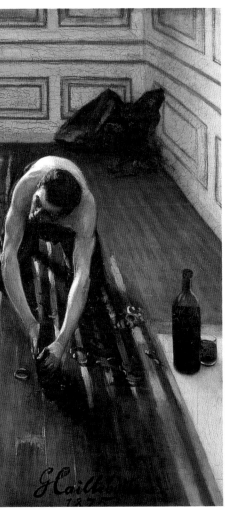

THE ART OF HIS DAY

Early in his career Cézanne exhibited alongside artists such as Manet, Whistler and Pissarro. In 1877 Cézanne showed 16 paintings at the third Impressionist exhibition which was received with a torrent of criticism. Unlike many of his contemporaries Cézanne spent a great deal of time away from Paris, often in his home town of Aix and the nearby Mediterranean village of L'Estaque. Meanwhile fellow Paris-based artists such as Monet, Degas and Manet continued to defy the critics with their determination to pursue the new style of painting and sweep away the traditional values of art. Manet's paintings of naked women depicted in recognisable settings shocked a public who were used to art which placed them in the socially acceptable realm of classical mythology. Degas' abrupt framing of everyday scenes copied the photographic 'snapshot' which was challenging art as a visual record. Monet's *Impression* of a sunrise over water with bold daubs of orange paint was ridiculed by critics whose description of the painting christened the Impressionist movement. Cézanne became increasingly influential himself as he developed his own style alongside the Post-Impressionist artists such as van Gogh, Gauguin and Seurat.

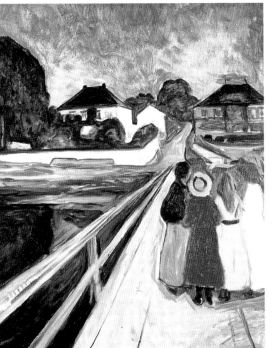

LITTLE DANCER OF FOURTEEN YEARS

Edgar Degas

This sculpture originally modelled in wax incorporates real artefacts such as hair, dancing shoes, gauze tutu and silk bodice. It was modelled on Marie van Goethem, a dancer at the Paris Opera, who was known to spend much of her time at the local Brasserie de Martyrs, also favoured by artists. The incorporation of real materials in the sculpture was considered very shocking at the time. It was finally exhibited, in a glass case, at the sixth Impressionist exhibition.

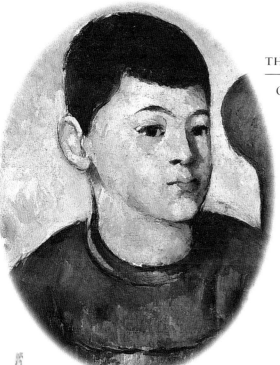

On 4 January 1872 in Paris, Hortense Fiquet gave birth to a boy who was registered as Paul Cézanne. The artist was an indulgent father who was very attached to his young son. As Paul grew up Cézanne began to depend upon him to help organise his affairs. He was later to become Cézanne's advisor, taking care of money matters and the sale of his pictures.

THE LIFE OF CÉZANNE

~1869~

Meets Hortense Fiquet, who models for him, and becomes his mistress

Hortense moves in with Cézanne

~1872~

Son Paul is born

Cézanne, Hortense and Paul move to the village of Auvers-sur-Oise where Cézanne works with Pissarro

~1874~

Exhibits with the first group exhibition of Impressionist painters

~1877~

Exhibits 16 paintings at the third Impressionist exhibition

~1878~

Cézanne's father threatens to cut off the artist's allowance after hearing of his son's mistress and child whom Cézanne had kept a secret

THE ARTIST'S
FATHER
(detail), 1866

In 1874, already two years after the birth of his son, Cézanne wrote to his parents; *'You ask me why I am not yet returning to Aix. I have already told you in that respect that it is more agreeable for me than you can possibly think to be with you, but that once at Aix I am no longer free and when I want to return to Paris this always means a struggle for me; and although your opposition to my return is not absolute, I am very much troubled by the resistance I feel on your part. I greatly desire that my liberty of action should not be impeded and I shall then have all the more pleasure in hastening my return. I ask Papa to give me 200 francs a month; that will permit me to make a long stay in Aix... believe me, I really do beg Papa to grant me this request and then I shall, I think, be able to continue the studies I wish to make.'*

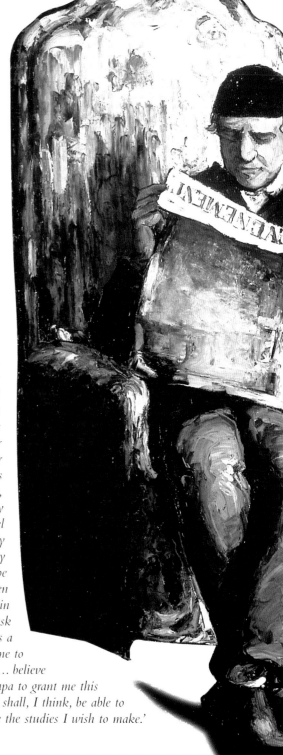

FAMILY, FRIENDS & OTHERS
THE SECRET FAMILY

Cézanne relied heavily on his wealthy parents for financial support. When he moved in with his lover Hortense Fiquet he kept the relationship a secret for fear that his father would cut off his monthly allowance. Cézanne continued to rely upon the financial and emotional support of his family for many years and evidently found it difficult to break free. He secretly established his family in l'Estaque, not far from his parents home in Aix, and continued to spend time with his parents as well as with Hortense, all the time fearful that he would be discovered. Cézanne was also close to his two sisters who shared the promise of the family wealth with him after his father retired from the banking business.

The secret of Hortense, and even the birth of Cézanne's son Paul, was kept from his parents but eventually they found out some eight years after Cézanne first met Hortense. Cézanne's father threatened to cut off his son's allowance, forcing Cézanne to seek support from his friends.

MADAME CÉZANNE
IN A RED DRESS, *c.*1890

Cézanne met the 19-year-old Hortense Fiquet in Paris in 1869. Hortense was a young model described as '*a tall and handsome brunette with large black eyes*'. Cézanne, some 11 years her senior, fell in love with her and persuaded her to move in with him. They were not married until 1886, when Cézanne was 47 and his son Paul 14. Although they stayed together for many years, eventually Cézanne became indifferent to her. After his father's death Cézanne continued to live with his mother and sister Marie in Aix, while Hortense spent most of her time in Paris with their son Paul. One scornful comment gives a good picture of Cézanne's attitude; '*My wife likes only Switzerland and lemonade,*' he said.

THE ARTIST'S LIFE
FAMILY, FRIENDS & OTHERS
FRIENDS FROM AIX

Throughout his life Cézanne maintained friends from his home town of Aix. The 'inseparables', the childhood friends Baille, Zola and Cézanne, kept their friendship going into adulthood. Émile Zola remained very close to Cézanne until a book published by Zola in 1886 offended Cézanne to such an extent that he ceased to communicate with the writer. The acquaintances Cézanne made at the drawing school in Aix where he studied from 1856 to 1859 lasted many years. When Cézanne left for Paris in pursuit of Zola who had already decided to make a home there, he found familiar faces from Aix such as Solari and Valabrègue. These young hopefuls rubbed shoulders with the exciting avant-garde in the Parisian cafes where artists and intellectuals debated the latest artistic fashions long into the night.

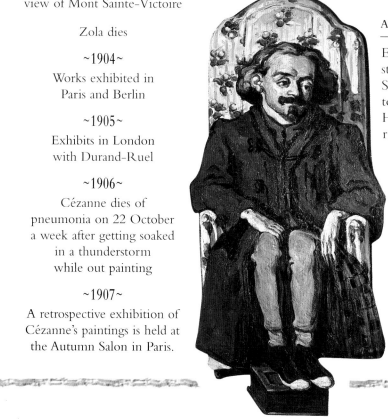

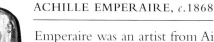

ACHILLE EMPERAIRE, c.1868

Emperaire was an artist from Aix who studied with Cézanne at the Académie Suisse in Paris. Cézanne was very attached to Emperaire who suffered from dwarfism. His painting portrays Emperaire's condition ruthlessly – the young man's feet are propped on a box because they would not reach the ground. However there is a sensitive handling of the face which shows Emperaire gazing thoughtfully into the distance. Emperaire stayed with Cézanne in Paris in 1872, but only for a short time. When he left he wrote; *'I have left Cézanne – it was unavoidable, otherwise I would not have escaped the fate of the others. I found him deserted by everybody. He hasn't got a single intelligent or close friend left.'* Later in life Cézanne is reported to have wanted to destroy the picture.

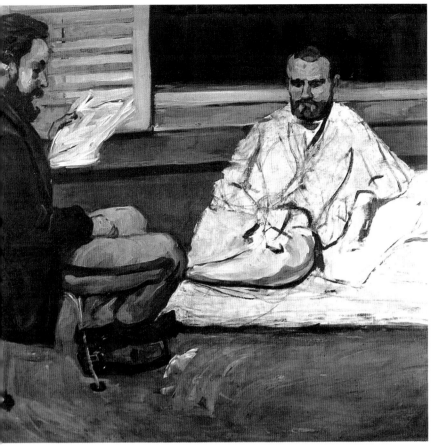

Zola and Cézanne had been
intimate friends since childhood.
Zola, a highly talented writer,
became notorious for his
Realist novels such as *Nana*
and *Germinal,* which although
causing a scandal when they were
published, today are considered to
be among the greatest French
novels of the 19th century. This
painting, found in Zola's attic
after his death, is clearly
unfinished, showing Zola's body
as a few bold brushstrokes against
the cream canvas. In 1886 Zola
published a novel called *L'Oeuvre*
about a failed painter named
Claude Lantier. The character
was said to be based on Cézanne.
This caused a permanent break
between the two and their
friendship never recovered.

On 4 April 1886 Cézanne wrote:

> *My dear Émile*
>
> *I have just received* L'Oeuvre, *which you were good enough to
> send me. I thank the author of* Les Rougon-Macquart *for
> this kind token of remembrance and ask him to permit me
> to clasp his hand while thinking of bygone years. Ever yours
> under the impulse of past times.*
>
> *Paul Cézanne*

The letter undoubtedly refers to the relationship in the past
tense and is far more formal than his normal letters to the writer.
Some years later Zola said; *'Ah yes, Cézanne. How I regret not having
been able to push him. In my Claude Lantier I have drawn a likeness of him
that is actually too mild, for if I had wanted to tell all…!'*

JOACHIM GASQUET, 1896/7

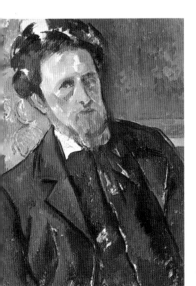

Gasquet was a young poet from Aix
and the son of one of Cézanne's
childhood friends. Gasquet
was very taken with
Cézanne's work and set
about publishing
transcriptions of lengthy
conversations he had
with the artist. After a
time their relationship
became strained, as was
the case with many of
Cézanne's friendships.

WHAT DO THE PAINTINGS SAY?

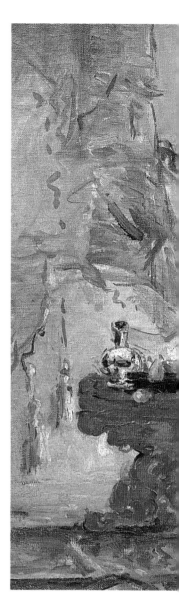

*S*udden outbursts of wild painting characterised Cézanne's work in the 1860s and early 70s. It is difficult to understand how this fits with the rest of his work but when Cézanne's friend Zola wrote the controversial book *L'Oeuvre*, which was thought to be based on Cézanne, he said of Claude Lantier (the main character of the novel): '*It was a chaste man's passion for the flesh of women, a mad love of nudity desired and never possessed…Those girls whom he chased out of his studio he adored in his paintings; he caressed or attacked them, in tears of despair at not being able to make them sufficiently beautiful, sufficiently alive.*'

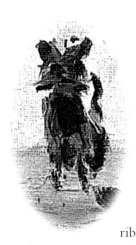

The black maid in attendance in Manet's painting has a far more active role in Cézanne's picture as she unveils the female figure to the man seated in the foreground.

Manet's *Olympia* includes a black cat representing promiscuity. The cat replaces the dog painted in Titian's version of Venus, which represented faithfulness. Cézanne includes a lapdog complete with red ribbon which suggests decadence.

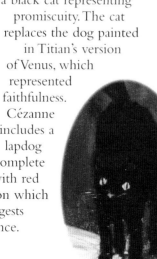

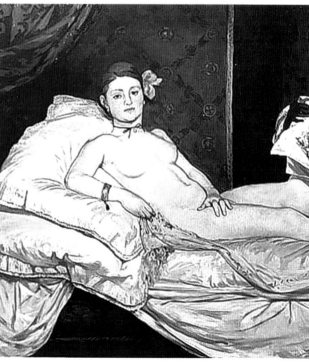

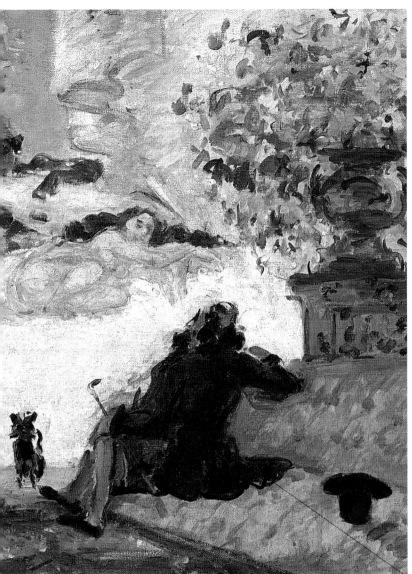

In 1867 Cézanne made a painting which he called *A Modern Olympia*. This painting was a homage to Manet's famous painting *Olympia* which was the sensation of the 1865 Salon. Apparently the subject came up in conversation some years later when Cézanne was staying with Dr. Gachet in Auvers. The story states that Cézanne immediately took up his brushes and with uncharacteristic speed painted another canvas also called *A Modern Olympia*. This version of 1873 was exhibited at the first Impressionist exhibition in 1874. Criticism was heaped upon the exhibition. A female critic who wrote in the paper *L'Artiste* under the name Marc de Montifaud commented of *A Modern Olympia*; *'On Sunday the public saw fit to sneer at a fantastic figure that is revealed under an opium sky to a drug addict. This apparition of pink and nude flesh... has left even the most courageous gasping for breath. Mr Cézanne merely gives the impression of being a sort of madman who paints in delirium tremens.'*

OLYMPIA

Édouard Manet

Manet painted *Olympia* in 1863 but did not submit it for exhibition until 1865. Manet referred back to a well-known painting called *Venus of Urbino* painted by Titian in 1538. Manet's Olympia is a modern courtesan who is self-possessed and confident, unashamed of her nakedness. She looks directly at the viewer, thereby involving the spectator in the scene. This confrontation was shocking for the public, who were used to gazing on images of naked women safely portrayed as mythical goddesses.

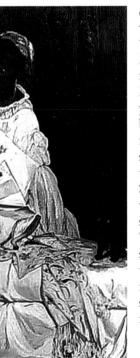

This man is undoubtedly a self-portrait with Cézanne's own distinct features.

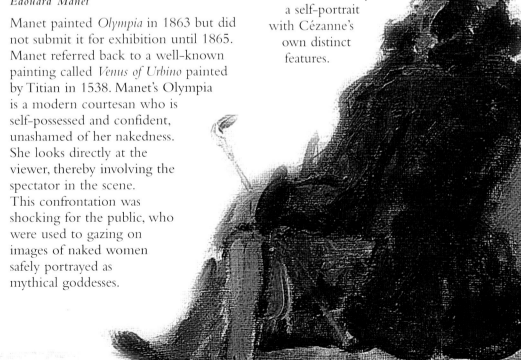

WHAT DO THE PAINTINGS SAY?
MONT SAINTE-VICTOIRE

The mountain of Sainte-Victoire dominates the landscape around Aix. Mont Sainte-Victoire became Cézanne's *motif*, his subject to which he continually returned, painting the landscape again and again. It is perhaps for his views of Sainte-Victoire that Cézanne is best known. In 1881 Cézanne's brother-in-law, Maxime Conil, purchased a house called Bellevue which stood to the southwest of the town of Aix. The house was situated on a hill overlooking the Arc valley with the mountain of Saint-Victoire in the distance. Cézanne visited Bellevue on many occasions, setting up his canvas to paint the rural landscape, especially the view along the valley towards the flat-topped mountain. A viaduct in the middle distance formed a bold horizontal line running towards the foot of the mountain. Cézanne loved this countryside which he had known so well since childhood. He said that the subject was '*the conformation of my country*,'

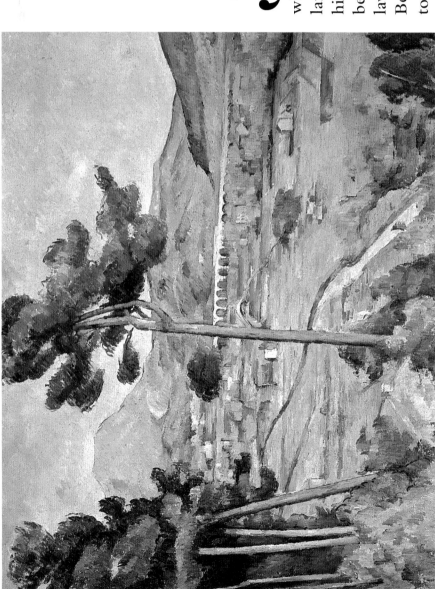

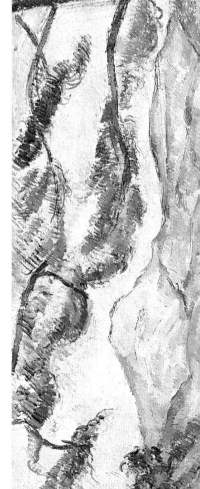

Mont Sainte-Victoire 1880

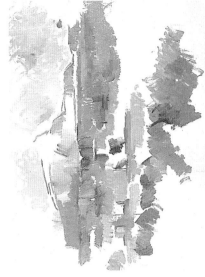

Cézanne painted Sainte-Victoire repeatedly in different conditions of light, exploring the form which appeared ever-changing under the harsh Provençal sun. However Cézanne's obsession was about making something with a strong underlying structure. He grew further and further away from the Impressionist painters whose fixation with the transient effects of light on colour was for Cézanne 'not permanent'. In conversation Cézanne said to Joachim Gasquet; *'Impressionism, what does it mean? It is the optical mixing of colours, do you understand? The colours are broken down on the canvas and reassembled by the eye. We had to go through that... but now we need to give a firmness, a framework to the evanescence of all things.'*

Mont Sainte-Victoire was the subject Cézanne chose to create this firmness, this permanence that he felt had eluded fellow painters such as Monet. It was more than just a mountain, itself the very essence of permanence. Sainte-Victoire was the foundation of Cézanne's beloved Provence countryside, the security of his family home, the solidity of his youthful friendships.

MONT SAINTE-VICTOIRE SEEN FROM LES LAUVES

When his last link with his parents was cut after his mother's death in 1897 Cézanne was drawn nearer to the mountain, taking a studio in the hills at Chemin des Lauves overlooking Aix. This painting made between 1904 and 1906 is a view of Sainte-Victoire from Les Lauves. The same motif Cézanne was painting almost 30 years earlier became increasingly abstract, with sky and ground merging together as Cézanne searched for the underlying framework in his painting.

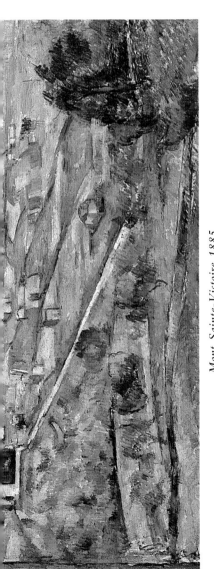

Mont Sainte-Victoire 1885

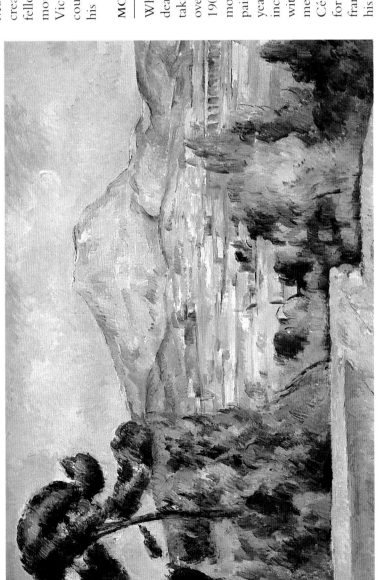

Mont Sainte-Victoire 1890

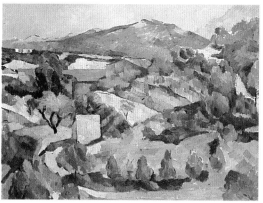

MOUNTAINS IN PROVENCE,
1878/80

Cézanne described how
he tried to paint from nature.
This description is a telling insight
into the way the artist works, his
thought process as he struggles to
create a work of art. *'If I reach too
high or too low, everything is a mess.*

*There must not be a single loose
strand, a single gap through which the
tension, the light, the truth can escape.
I have all the parts of my canvas under
control simultaneously. If things are
tending to diverge, I use my instincts
and my beliefs to bring them back
together again…I take the tones of
colour I see to my right and my left,
here, there everywhere, and I fix these
gradations, I bring them together…
They form lines, and become objects,
rocks, trees, without my thinking
about it. They acquire volume, they
have an effect. When these masses and
weights on my canvas correspond to the
planes, and spots which I see in my
mind and which we see with our eyes,
then my canvas closes its fingers.'*

HOW WERE THEY MADE?
THE STRUCTURE OF THINGS

Cézanne was reaching for a way of painting what was beneath the surface, the basic form of his subject expressed and modelled in colour. His fellow Impressionist painters worked very quickly in order to capture the fleeting impression of light on the surface whereas Cézanne worked slowly, laboriously, using colour to build solid shapes. He is famous for his statement that he *'wanted to make of Impressionism something solid and durable, like the art of the Museums.'*

He sought to create images which represented the subject as colour and tone together, that is to identify a colour which could represent the tone of an object and in this way build something solid out of colour alone, without the need for line or shade. He expressed this method of working when he said; *'I try to render perspective through colour alone…'I proceed very slowly, for nature reveals herself to me in a very complex form, and constant progress must be made. One must see one's model correctly and experience it in the right way, and furthermore, express oneself with distinction and strength.'*

BEND IN THE ROAD,
*c.*1900/6

Cézanne increasingly analyzed his landscapes as ordered brushstrokes and parallel colour blocks which are described today as *'constructive strokes'.* Through these building blocks of colour he attempted to represent sunlight on the landscape rather than provide an impression of its effects. Although he rejected the Impressionist style he still adopted the use of complementary colours famously used by the Impressionists, such as setting muted blues against oranges to create depth in the picture plane. It is in canvases such as *Bend in the Road* and the 1904 painting of *Sainte-Victoire* (see page 17) that historians have seen the beginnings of Cubist and eventually Abstract art.

PAUL CÉZANNE
SITTING IN
THE COUNTRY

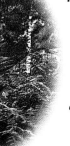

This photograph,
taken by Cézanne's
friend Émile Bernard,
shows Cézanne as an
old man in his beloved
Provençale countryside.

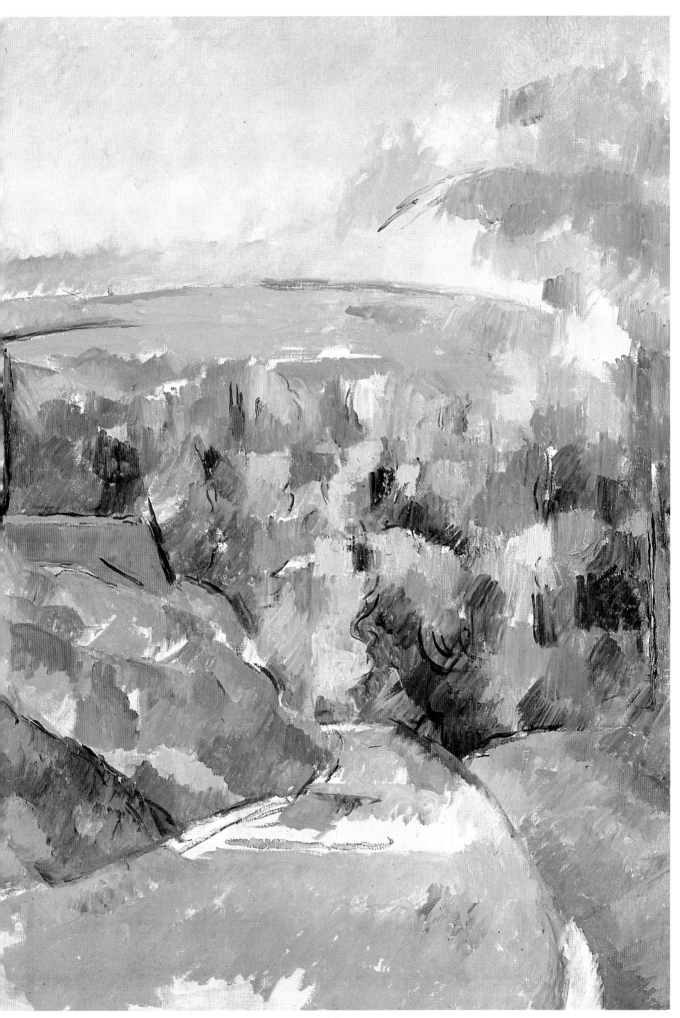

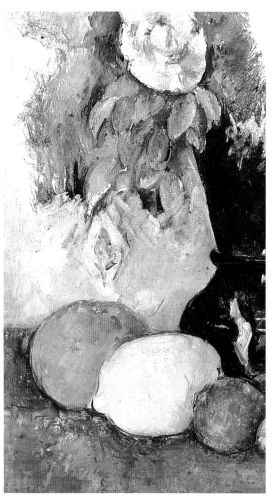

FLOWERS AND FRUITS, *c*.1880

Cézanne derived enormous pleasure
from creating fruits which were painted
with such delicacy of colour and yet
were given real volume and weight.
It is almost as if the viewer can feel
their roundness in the palm of the hand.

HOW WERE THEY MADE?

STILL LIFE

Cézanne said he wanted to conquer Paris with an apple – in other words to become famous for his modest still-life paintings. He applied the same methodical analysis to his still-life pictures as he did to his landscapes which often resulted in the fruit rotting in the bowl before he could finish the painting, so eventually he used artificial fruit. The simple shapes of the fruit and bowls appealed to him; they were after all the basic spheres, cubes and cylinders out of which all things can be said to be made. Another indication of the time he devoted to the paintings is the fact that sometimes contradicting shadows can be seen. Each time he returned to the subject he would paint exactly what he saw, even if the shadow had moved. He would spend weeks, sometimes months or longer on a painting, and if he was not happy with the result would abandon the picture or sometimes destroy it.

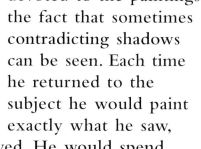

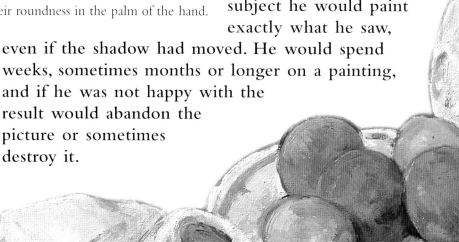

VESSELS, BASKET AND FRUIT, 1888/90

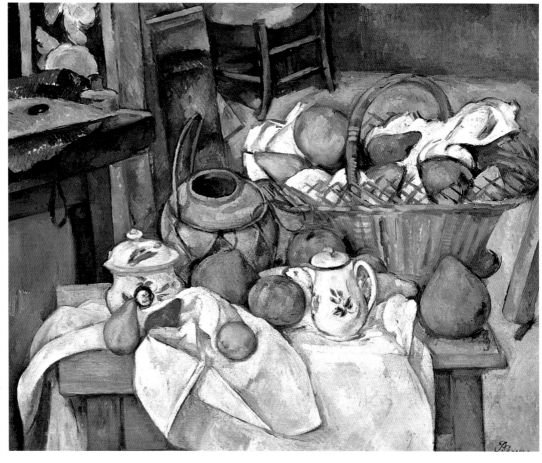

The still-life pictures appear at first glance to be simple representations of everyday objects, and yet these paintings are some of the most sophisticated images to have been created at the end of the 19th century. The artist's viewpoint has been very carefully selected and is in fact not one but several shifting viewpoints. The objects are seen from a number of different angles at the same time, so the jug appears to be tipping forward but the plane of the table top contradicts it. The distortions of perspective are deliberate so that important shapes and colours balance each other pictorially rather than present a true representation of the still life. This playfulness broke with the rules of art which had been established for generations and stretched back to the Renaissance. Cézanne flattens the perspective where it pleases him to do so, pursuing harmony of shape and colour to create a painting which cares more for the 'abstract' elements of composition than for a perfect illusion of objects on a table.

STILL LIFE WITH CURTAIN, c.1898/9

This still life was carefully arranged in order to present exactly the combination of shapes and juxtaposition of colours that Cézanne wanted.

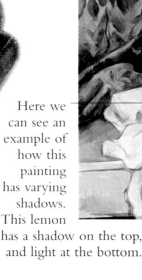

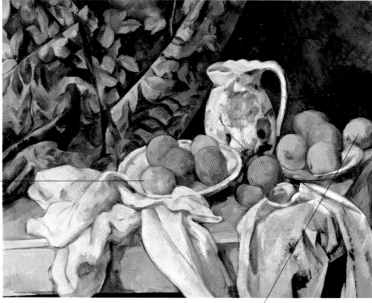

Here we can see an example of how this painting has varying shadows. This lemon has a shadow on the top, and light at the bottom.

The shadow and light are reversed here.

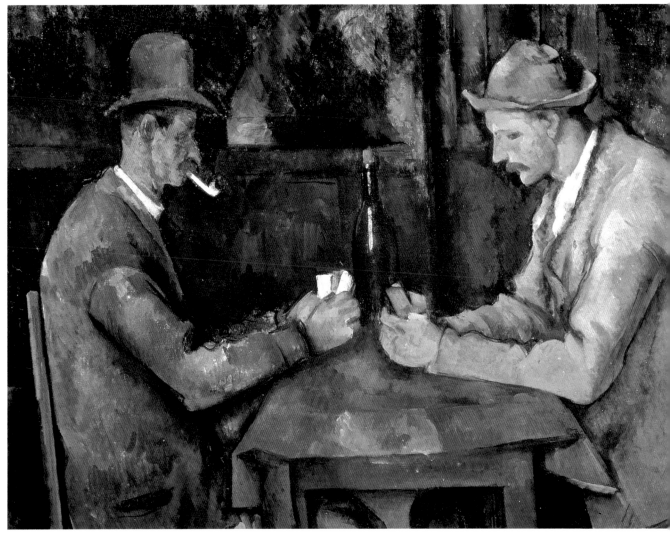

THE CARD PLAYERS, 1890/95

The Card Players is one of Cézanne's best-known works. Card players are a common subject for artists and many versions of such a scene existed before Cézanne set up his canvas. He made five versions of the scene in all. Rather like his still-life pictures and paintings of Sainte-Victoire he painted the subject again and again exploring variations of the theme. In one version only two players are depicted, facing each other. In another three players sit around the table while another has three players, a standing onlooker and a boy at the shoulder of the central card player.

SOMBRE COLOURS

We can tell from the simple clothes that the figures clearly belong in the Provençale countryside and their serious expressions suggest they have a hard life. This rather gloomy atmosphere is emphasised by the sombre colours used by the artist.

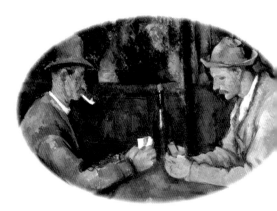

ABSTRACT QUALITIES OF THE IMAGE

The very symmetrical composition with eyes focused down on the cards gives the pictures a stillness which recalls Cézanne's still-life paintings. Cézanne's arrangement of people and prop-like objects is organised in a manner which deliberately sets out to present a combination of shapes and colours rather than tell the story of two men playing cards. The artist is more interested in the abstract qualities of the image than a representation of an event.

FAMOUS IMAGES

*A*fter the death of his father in 1886 Cézanne inherited a large fortune and he could have led whatever life he chose. He decided on the simple life at Jas de Bouffan, the family house in Aix, painting the surrounding countryside and whatever was close at hand. Cézanne often found models for his portrait paintings among the labourers who worked on the estate at Jas de Bouffan. He could afford to pay these workers to sit for him for long periods of time, for Cézanne was as exacting with his studies of people as he was with the still life and landscape. He painted at Jas de Bouffan, living an increasingly secluded life with his sister as well as Hortense and Paul, until he set up a new studio on the road to Les Lauves which afforded views of his favourite motif, Mont Sainte-Victoire. It appeared that Cézanne increasingly shunned contact with people, sometimes positively ducking out of sight of acquaintances he might meet in the street.

WOMAN WITH A COFFEE POT, 1890/5

It is likely that the subject for this painting was one of the servants at Jas de Bouffan, possibly the housekeeper. There is a feeling of massiveness about the form of the woman, a sense that the figure is as monumental as the mountain outside Aix that Cézanne loved to paint.

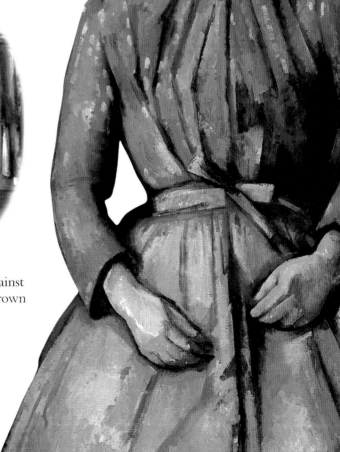

The vertical forms of the cafetière and standing spoon echo the erect pose of the woman who appears to be painted in a different plane to the table top, just as Cézanne painted conflicting perspectives in his still-life pictures.

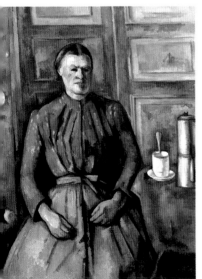

The blues and greens of the woman's dress against the orange and burnt brown of the wall panelling and tablecloth tend to accentuate her solidity and isolate her from the background.

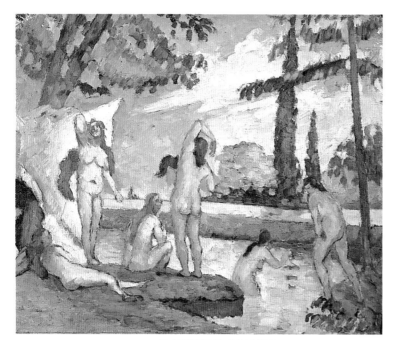

BATHERS, 1875/77

This is one of the earliest examples of Cézanne's
paintings of bathers in the landscape.

FAMOUS IMAGES
THE BATHERS

*I*n 1899 the Jas de Bouffan was sold and Cézanne moved into an apartment in Aix with a housekeeper. His wife and son spent most of their time in Paris, and Cézanne had a house built at Chemin des Lauves in the hills outside Aix. The house had a studio on the first floor with a ceiling some five metres high and a long narrow slit in the outer wall in order to move large canvases. Around 1900 Cézanne returned to a favourite subject, figures in the landscape. He had painted a number of paintings on this theme in the 1870s and 80s but he now concentrated on making a number of large paintings including the biggest canvas at over two metres by two and a half metres.

THE LARGE BATHERS, 1894-1905

This group of bathers comprises all female figures, like the other large bathers canvas. Cézanne did not mix male and female bathers together in his pictures, possibly for fear of creating a scene which would be considered inappropriate, and which would distract from his main purpose of using the figures as compositional devices, completely anonymous as human beings. However symbolic elements have been introduced into the picture and it is certain that Cézanne would have been aware of their meaning. The dog, curled up asleep at the foot of the picture, represents faithfulness. The fruit on the ground and in the basket represent the loss of innocence. These symbols have been used for centuries, and Cézanne himself used similar references in earlier works including *The Modern Olympia* (see page 15) which was based on a painting by Manet.

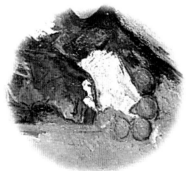

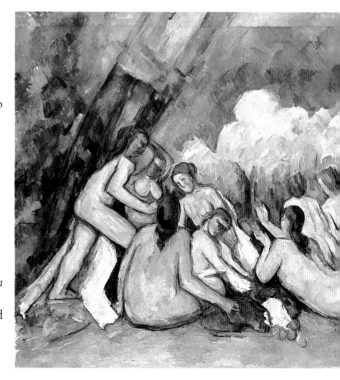

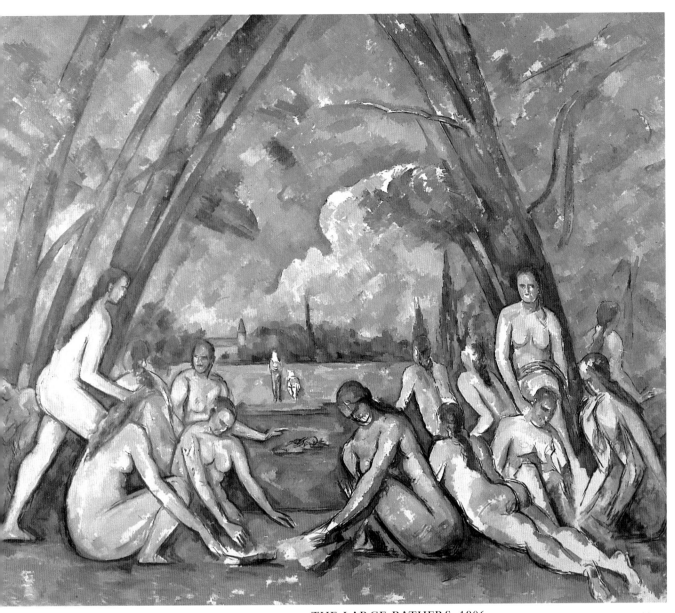

THE LARGE BATHERS, 1906

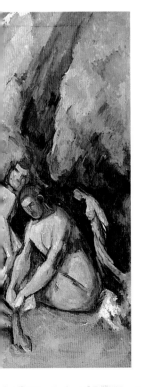

Cézanne spent seven years working on this painting in his methodical manner, returning to the canvas on numerous occasions in order to change aspects, or to add a little, just as he did with all his paintings. The canvas, which is now in the Museum of Art in Philadelphia, was the largest Cézanne painted. It has a strong triangular-shaped centre emphasised by the leaning figures and trees, and comprises a group of women - no men are present – who appear to be resting after bathing. The women are crudely depicted, and are more important for the structural shapes they present than for their individuality.

At the centre of the triangle on the far side of the river are two figures and behind them a church tower. One of the figures standing on the far bank is a man with his arms folded, staring across at the women. It has been suggested that this is Cézanne himself, under the shadow of the church, looking across the river at the women, at a scene he can never reach. Several of the women are staring back towards the figure. Is this a comment on his relationship with women from whom he grew more distant as life progressed?

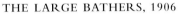

25

HOW WERE THEY MADE?
THE BATHERS

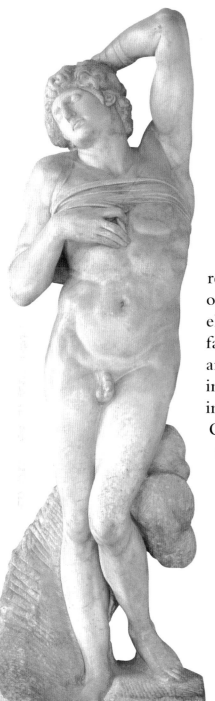

ézanne would draw figures from life, although he became increasingly awkward with models, especially in unclothed poses. Instead he started to rely upon memory and references taken from sketches and reproductions of paintings from the Old Masters in the Louvre and elsewhere, even sketches from illustrations in his sister's fashion magazines. One report mentions Cézanne using an album entitled *Le Nu au Musée du Louvre* (The nude in the Louvre Museum), which he bought from a shop in Paris as a reference for figure studies. Wherever Cézanne did make studies from life he would use and reuse the figure in many works, treating it as a stock item which could be called upon for a number of different purposes.

A PHENOMENAL MEMORY

For his bathers series Cézanne relied on his memory of the human form to help him create the figures. *'Painting is in here'* he said, tapping his head. Critics have found clear references in the Bathers series to known works such as Michelangelo's *Dying Slave* sculpture (above).

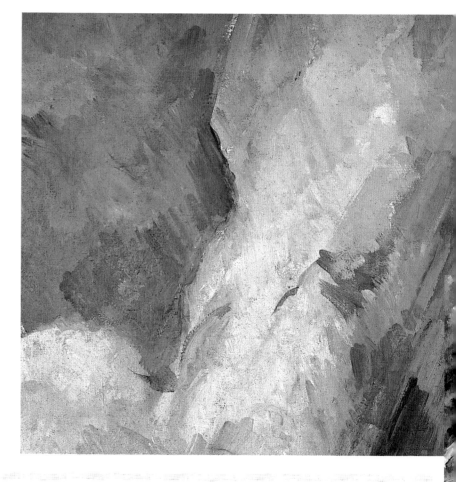

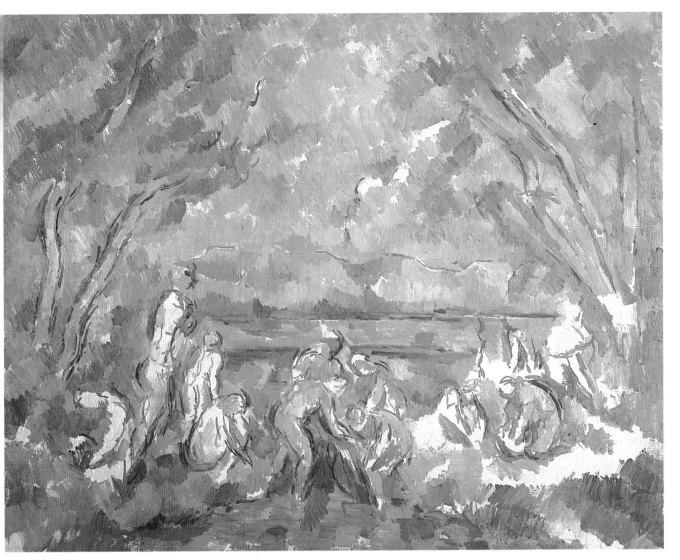

BATHERS

In addition to the canvases painted in oils he produced a number of pencil and watercolour sketches dominated by blues and greys. These did not serve as preparatory sketches for the oil paintings but are independent versions in their own right. Some of the watercolour and oil paintings appear unfinished because Cézanne has left areas of the paper or canvas uncovered so the base colour shows through. It is almost as if the act of filling in the canvas would have unbalanced the picture, and that the spots of white are as important as the patches of colour in creating an overall harmony. This painting demonstrates the 'hatching' brushstrokes that Cézanne frequently used, going in different directions to provide movement across the picture surface.

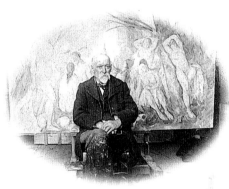

Cézanne in front of one of the Large Bathers

THE LARGE BATHERS – DETAIL

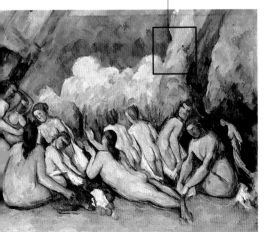

This detail from the sky of *The Large Bathers* (page 25) shows the way in which Cézanne applied the paint. Loose, large brushstrokes have been used to apply fairly thin coats of pigment in a very free style. The contra-angled strokes are clearly visible in this detail, and serve to animate the picture's surface when seen from a distance. The picture gives the appearance of being painted quickly although it is known that Cézanne spent literally years working on the canvas.

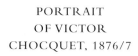

THE AUDIENCE FOR THE PICTURES

Cézanne exhibited with the Impressionists during the 1870s and at small shows such as Les Vingt in Brussels but did not have his own exhibition until 1895, when his work was exhibited at the gallery of Paris art dealer Ambroise Vollard. Cézanne did not need to sell his paintings to make a living as he was financially independent after the death of his father. His work was exhibited sporadically during the late 1890s and an auction of Émile Zola's art collection on his death in 1902 saw Cézanne's paintings fetch an average of 1,500 francs. The first gallery to buy his work was the Nationalgalerie in Berlin. Shortly before his death in 1906 the art world was beginning to take notice of Cézanne's work, with 30 paintings being displayed in the 1904 Paris Salon and 10 paintings being exhibited at the Grafton Street gallery in London in 1905, thanks to the efforts of dealer Durand-Ruel. In 1907, the year after Cézanne's death, a major retrospective exhibition of his work featuring 56 paintings was held at the Paris Autumn Salon.

PORTRAIT OF VICTOR CHOCQUET, 1876/7

Victor Chocquet was a civil servant in the Ministry of Finance who was not wealthy, but nevertheless became a collector of art after befriending the Impressionist painters. Cézanne painted his portrait many times. Chocquet built up an impressive collection of paintings including 35 works by Cézanne.

DARK AND LEGENDARY

The art critic Gustave Geffroy (left) saw the exhibition organised by Ambroise Vollard and wrote the following; *'Passers-by walking into the Galerie Vollard, in rue Laffitte, will be faced with about 50 pictures: figures, landscapes, fruit, flowers, from which they can finally reach a verdict on one of the finest and greatest personalities of our time. Once that has happened, and it is high time it did happen, all that is dark and legendary about Cézanne's life will disappear, and what remains will be a rigorous and yet attractive, masterly and yet naive life's work… He will end up in the Louvre.'*

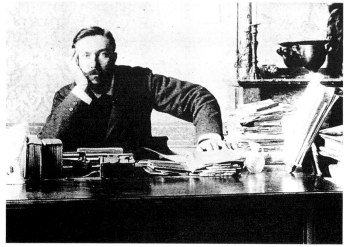

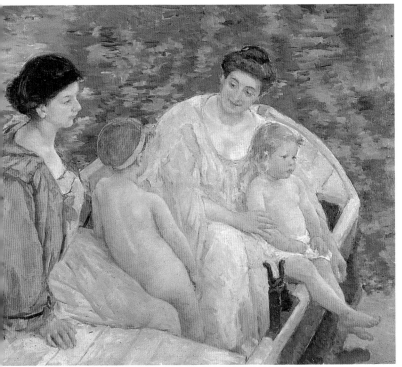

THE BATH, *c*.1881

Mary Cassatt

The American Impressionist painter Mary Cassatt met Cézanne in 1894 when they were both staying at Claude Monet's home town of Giverny. She describes her first encounter with Cézanne; *'When I first saw him, he looked like a cut-throat with large red eyeballs standing out from his head in a most ferocious manner, a rather fierce-looking pointed beard, quite grey, and an excited way of talking that positively made the dishes rattle...in spite of the total disregard for the dictionary of manners, he shows a politeness towards us which no other man here would have shown.'*

ORTRAIT OF AMBROISE VOLLARD *(left detail)*, 1889

A young art dealer named Ambroise Vollard who had made contact with Cézanne through his son Paul decided to champion Cézanne's work. He arranged a one-man exhibition of Cézanne's paintings in his Paris gallery in 1895, exhibiting 50 works to a public who knew nothing of this painter from Aix.

SELF-PORTRAIT *(detail)*, 1873/6

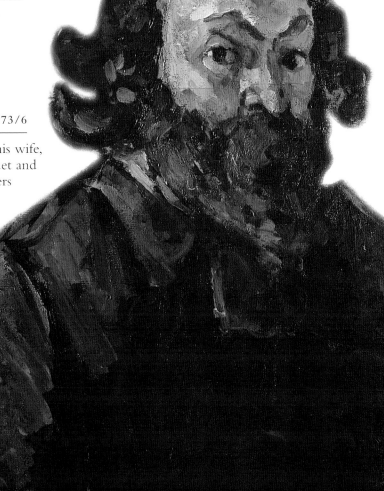

Cézanne painted the portraits of his wife, his son, friends such as Zola and Gasquet and sometimes the servants and labourers around the family estate, but did not undertake commissions in the same way as his contemporaries such as Renoir did. Cézanne did not need the money from such commissions but also his very slow and methodical way of working did not lend itself to private sittings. The artist painted his own portrait repeatedly, one model he could guarantee would pose without problems, unlike his young son who could never stay still to the satisfaction of his father. This self-portrait was made around 1875. The critic Louis Vauxcelles described Cézanne in an article; *'Cézanne is a legendary figure with a coarse bristly face, a body wrapped in a haulier's rough woollen greatcoat. But this Cézanne is a master.'*

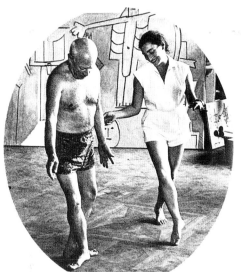

THE ARTIST'S INFLUENCE

A LASTING IMPRESSION

THE FATHER OF US ALL

Cézanne was described by Picasso (shown left with Jaqueline Roque) as *'My one and only master... Cézanne was like the father of us all.'*

Cézanne's art is considered today to be of profound importance to the development of Western art in the 20th century. Historians point to Cézanne's search for the underlying structure in his compositions as the foundation of modern art from which Cubism and then Abstraction came. He has never been considered an Impressionist painter despite being one of that small group who first exhibited a new way of painting which was so shocking to its public. It is above all Cézanne's obsession with formal elements of composition and his use of colour as tone rather than the Impressionist pursuit of light on surface that makes his art so important to those who followed. Cézanne's work made it possible for artists to start to question what they saw, the way in which they saw it, and how they interpreted and represented what was in front of them.

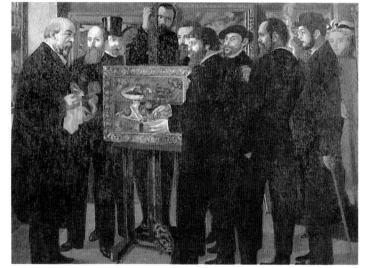

HOMAGE TO CÉZANNE

Maurice Denis

Many artists of different persuasion found something to admire in Cézanne. The Cubists such as Braque and also Picasso considered him the father of Cubism. Symbolist painters such as Gauguin and Maurice Denis looked to Cézanne's work as a source of inspiration even though Cézanne himself thought the Symbolist work too concerned with surface decoration. In 1900 Maurice Denis painted a homage to Cézanne. This painting shows a group of artists gathered round the Cézanne painting *Still Life with Compotier* which had once been owned by Paul Gauguin. Included in the picture are Maurice Denis and his wife, Odilon Redon, Pierre Bonnard, Édouard Vuillard, Paul Serusier and the art dealer Ambroise Vollard.

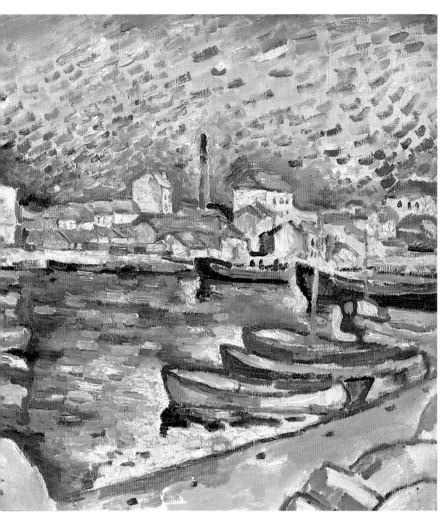

L'ESTAQUE

Georges Braque

In a letter to the artist Émile Bernard, Cézanne wrote; *'Treat nature by means of the cylinder, the sphere, the cone, with everything in its proper perspective so that each side of an object or plane is directed towards a central point. Lines parallel to the horizon give breadth, that is a section of nature… Lines perpendicular to this horizon give depth. But nature for us men is more depth than surface…'* This letter has become very famous because when Cézanne referred to seeing nature in terms of the basic shapes, it appeared that he was already looking at things in the Cubist's way. Cubist art first came to the public's attention in 1907 when Braque exhibited a painting at the Paris Salon and Matisse commented that he had reduced everything to little cubes. Cubism has been seen by art historians as the breaking point between representational art and abstract art that was to dominate the 20th century.

MONT SAINTE-VICTOIRE, 1905/6

A few weeks before he died Cézanne wrote to his son in Paris;
'I must tell you that as a painter I am becoming more clear-sighted before Nature, but with me the realization of my senses is always painful. I cannot attain the intensity that is unfolded before my senses. I do not have the magnificent richness of colouring that animates Nature.'

LES LAUVES

The studio that Cézanne had built at Les Lauves remains today as a small museum to the artist. Unfortunately it was not possible to preserve the view across to Sainte-Victoire which was so important to Cézanne – it is now obscured by apartment blocks.

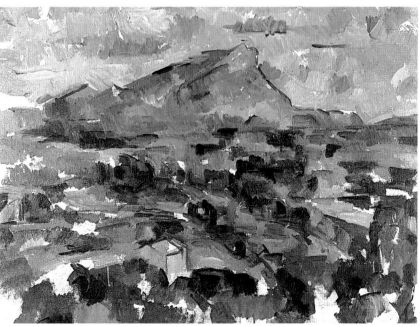

GLOSSARY

Sandro Botticelli (1445-1510) - An extremely influential painter who lived and worked in Florence at the end of the 15th century. His best-known works, such as *The Birth of Venus*, use both pagan and Christian imagery together, and are executed in a style which was soon to be displaced by the High Renaissance style of Michelangelo.

Hatching - This is shading by means of parallel lines on a drawing or painting. Cross-hatching is shading with two sets of parallel lines, one crossing the other. It is often used to depict shadows or dark tones rather than filling an area with solid colour.

Expressionism - The Expressionist movement in art sought a way to express emotional force through exaggerated line and colour. Expressionist painters turned from the naturalism found in Impressionist art and attempted to create emotional impact with strong colours and simplified forms such as those found in van Gogh's work.

Still life - The still life usually depicts a collection of objects (jugs, plates, flowers, fruit, candles etc.) which do not appear to be important in their own right but were usually chosen by the artist to symbolise more than their individual appearance. Items such as skulls, hourglasses, candles or butterflies were often depicted to represent the transient nature of life, for example, as were certain types of flowers known for their seasonality. The tradition started in about the 16th century.

Motif - This is a word which is used to describe a distinctive idea or theme which is continuously elaborated by the artist and applies to many kinds of art forms such as music, painting and literature. Cézanne's motif was Mont Sainte-Victoire, which he painted repeatedly during his lifetime.

Oeuvre - A French term which is used to describe the entire output of one artist. An Oeuvre catalogue, therefore, attempts to give a record of every work produced by the artist. The term can also apply to musicians and writers. Zola's book which caused a rift with Cézanne was entitled *L'Oeuvre*, and was a play on words.

ACKNOWLEDGEMENTS

Copyright © 2008 *ticktock* Entertainment Ltd.,
First published in Great Britain by *ticktock* Media Ltd.,
Unit 2, Orchard Business Centre, North Farm Road, Tunbridge Wells, Kent, TN2 3XF. All rights reserved.
No part of this publication may be reproduced, stored in a retrieval system, or transmitted in any form or by any means electronic, mechanical, photocopying, recording or otherwise, without prior written permission of the copyright owner.

A CIP catalogue record for this book is available from the British Library.
ISBN 978 1 84696 879 2
Printed in China
9 8 7 6 5 4 3 2 1

Picture Credits t=top, b=bottom, c=centre, l=left, r=right, OFC=outside front cover,
IFC=inside front cover, IBC=inside back cover, OBC=outside back cover.

AKG; 3r, 10r, 30tl. Bridgeman Art Library (London); 2tl, 8/9t, 22t & 22cr & 22bl & OBC, 26l, 28tl, 28bl, 28/29t, 30/31t. Giraudon; OFC (main pic), 2/3c & OFC, 4tl, 4/5b, 5t & 5br, 6tl, 6/7b, 6/7t, 8/9b, 10tl, 11r, 12cb & OBC, 12/13t, 13bl & 13br, 14bl & 14cl & 14/15t & 15br, 16bl, 16/17b, 17br, 17tr, 18tl, 19, 20tl, 20/21b & 21br & IFC, 21t, 23bl & 23c & 23br, 24tl, 24bl & 24/25b & 26br & 27bl, 25t & 25br, 28/29c, 29br, 30bl, 30/31c, 31br. Réunion des Musées Nationaux © RMN/R.G.Ojeda; 18cb, 27cr. Roger-Viollet © Harlingue-Viollet; 2cb. Roger-Viollet © Collection Viollet; 7br & 32ct. Tate Gallery (London); 9br,

Every effort has been made to trace the copyright holders and we apologise in advance for any unintentional omissions. We would be pleased to insert the appropriate acknowledgement in any subsequent edition of this publication.